E BIOG FUL

Whiting, Jim, 1943-

Robert Fulton

**Please check all items for damages
before leaving the Library.
Thereafter you will be held
responsible for all injuries
to items beyond reasonable wear.**

What's So Great About...?

ROBERT FULTON

Jim Whiting

P.O. Box 196
Hockessin, Delaware 19707
Visit us on the web: www.mitchelllane.com
Comments? email us: mitchelllane@mitchelllane.com

Mitchell Lane PUBLISHERS

Printing   1   2   3   4   5   6   7   8   9

A Robbie Reader/What's So Great About . . . ?

Annie Oakley	Daniel Boone	Davy Crockett
Ferdinand Magellan	Francis Scott Key	Henry Hudson
Jacques Cartier	Johnny Appleseed	**Robert Fulton**
Sam Houston		

Library of Congress Cataloging-in-Publication Data
Whiting, Jim, 1943–
    Robert Fulton / by Jim Whiting.
      p. cm. — (A Robbie Reader. What's so great about . . . ?)
    Includes bibliographical references and index.
    ISBN 1-58415-478-0 (library bound)
    1. Fulton, Robert, 1765–1815 — Juvenile literature. 2. Marine engineers — United States — Biography — Juvenile literature. 3. Inventors — United States — Biography — Juvenile literature. 4. Steamboats — United States — History — 19th century — Juvenile literature. I. Title. II. Series.
    VM140.F9W485 2006
    623.8'24092 — dc22

                                                              2006006116

ISBN-10: 1-58415-478-0   ISBN-13: 9781584154785

ABOUT THE AUTHOR: Jim Whiting has been a remarkably versatile and accomplished journalist, writer, editor, and photographer for more than 30 years. A voracious reader since early childhood, Mr. Whiting has written and edited about 200 nonfiction children's books. His subjects range from authors to zoologists and include contemporary pop icons and classical musicians, saints and scientists, emperors and explorers. Representative titles include *The Life and Times of Franz Liszt*, *The Life and Times of Julius Caesar*, *Charles Schulz*, *Charles Darwin and the Origin of the Species*, *Juan Ponce de Leon*, *Annie Oakley*, and *The Scopes Monkey Trial*.

He lives in Washington State with his wife and two teenage sons.

PHOTO CREDITS: Cover — Stock Montage/Getty Images; pp. 1, 3, 4, 10, 14, 18, 22 — Library of Congress; p. 8 — North Wind Picture Archives; p. 12 — Sharon Beck; p. 13 — Rosenthal; p. 17 — Royal Navy Museum; p. 20 — Roger Viollet/Getty Images; pp. 24, 25 — U.S. Naval Historical Center; p. 27 — Jamie Kondrchek.

PUBLISHER'S NOTE: The following story has been thoroughly researched and to the best of our knowledge represents a true story. While every possible effort has been made to ensure accuracy, the publisher will not assume liability for damages caused by inaccuracies in the data, and makes no warranty on the accuracy of the information contained herein.

                                                              PLB

A Robbie Reader

TABLE OF CONTENTS

Words in **bold** type can be found in the glossary.

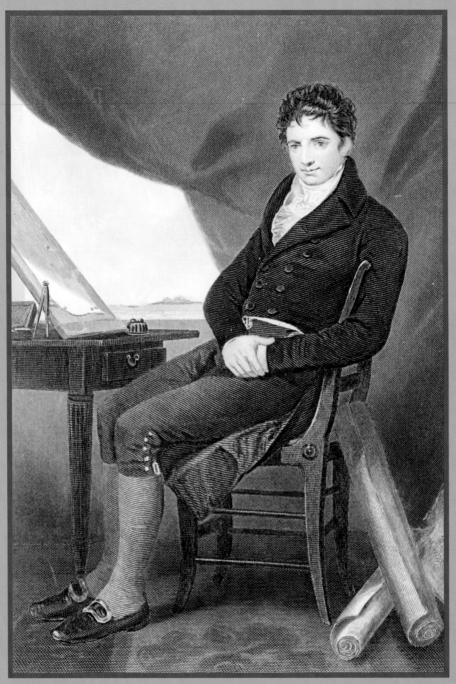

Robert Fulton invented many things, including a saw for cutting marble and a submarine. He was also a portrait painter, and he helped build canals. His most famous invention, however, would be his steamship.

"Fulton's Folly"

In August 1807, a new boat was ready for its first run up the Hudson River from New York City. It had attracted a lot of attention while it was being built. Other boats of that **era** were propelled by sails or by oars. This one was different. Steam provided its power.

Many people were afraid of the boat. Others thought that it would fail. They called it "Fulton's **Folly**."

The name came from its builder, Robert Fulton. Fulton was very confident in his boat. So was his business partner, Robert Livingston.

The two men thought that the boat could make regular trips from New York City to Albany. Albany was the capital of New York

Fulton's steamship traveled up the Hudson River from New York City to Albany. It passed many communities along the way, causing much excitement.

state. At that time, most people traveled by horseback or stagecoach. The trip was long and uncomfortable. If their boat was successful, it would make the trip shorter and more comfortable. It would also cost less than the stagecoach.

Finally everything was ready. Fulton started the engine.

For a few moments, the doubters appeared to be correct. The boat steamed a few feet from the dock and stopped.

Fulton disappeared below. He made some corrections. The engine started again. This time it ran perfectly.

The passage of the boat up the river caused a sensation. Some people thought it was a sea monster. Fulton arrived fourteen hours later at Clermont, Livington's **estate** (eh-STAYT) on the Hudson River. Many people believe that *Clermont* was also the name of Fulton's boat. It wasn't. He named it the *North River Steam Boat.*

The *North River Steam Boat* passes a large sailing vessel on its first voyage up the Hudson River. Friends of Robert Fulton and Robert Livingston wave to the sailors.

The boat left Clermont the next morning. Several hours later it arrived at Albany. The passengers got off. A few people got on for the return trip, which was just as uneventful as the trip upriver.

The boat averaged nearly five miles an hour. It was a high rate of speed for that time. The steamboat era in the United States was under way.

The trip had another benefit for Fulton. During the stop at Clermont, Fulton met Livington's cousin Harriet. The two were married in 1808. They would have four children.

Benjamin West was a famous painter. He was born in the United States and spent most of his life in England. Fulton would move to England to study painting with West.

Growing Up

Robert Fulton was born on November 14, 1765, on a farm in Little Britain Township, Pennsylvania. His parents were Robert and Mary Fulton. He had three older sisters: Belle, Betsy, and Polly. A younger brother, Abraham, would follow.

The farm failed when Robert was six. The Fultons moved to the town of Lancaster.

Two years later, Robert's father died. Somehow the family managed to make ends meet. That was important for Robert, because he was able to go to school. He could also pursue his hobbies. One was painting. Another was putting things together. He made his own pencils. He assembled a **skyrocket** for the

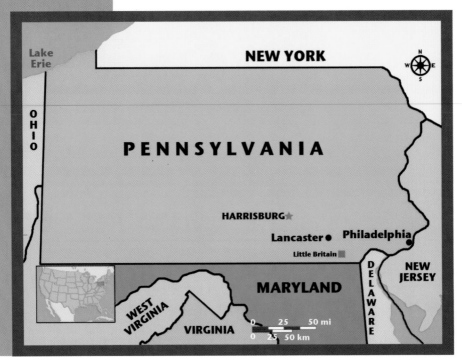

Robert Fulton was born in Little Britain and grew up in Lancaster, Pennsylvania. He moved to Philadelphia when he was 17.

Fourth of July celebration. He even invented hand-cranked paddle wheels for a small boat. The paddles made the boat go faster than using poles to push it.

Robert grew up during the Revolutionary War. There weren't any battles near Lancaster, but Robert saw lots of soldiers. Lancaster was an important center of supplies for the American troops.

One of Fulton's earliest successful inventions was the hand-cranked paddle wheels on this little boat. He experimented with them when he was about 14 years old.

He moved to Philadelphia at the age of 17. At first he worked for a jeweler. Then he opened his own jewelry shop. He also created tiny paintings. He must have done well in these businesses. When he was 21, he gave his mother enough money to buy a small farm.

Then he decided to go to London, England, to work with Benjamin West, a famous painter. Fulton didn't become very successful as an artist. He struggled to make a living for five years. He needed to do something else.

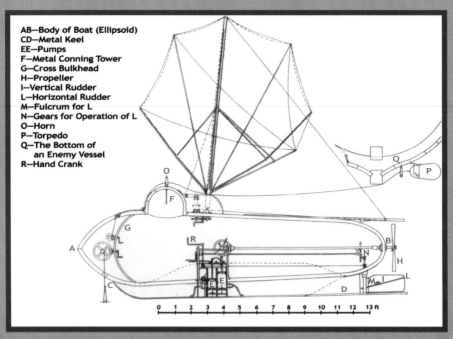

AB—Body of Boat (Ellipsoid)
CD—Metal Keel
EE—Pumps
F—Metal Conning Tower
G—Cross Bulkhead
H—Propeller
I—Vertical Rudder
L—Horizontal Rudder
M—Fulcrum for L
N—Gears for Operation of L
O—Horn
P—Torpedo
Q—The Bottom of
   an Enemy Vessel
R—Hand Crank

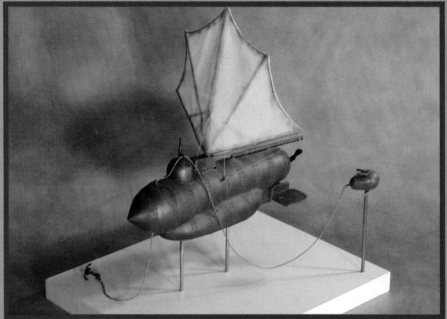

A diagram and model of Fulton's *Nautilus*, an early version of the submarine. The sail propelled the vessel when it was on the surface. A crew member operated a hand crank (R) to drive the boat when it was submerged. A torpedo (P) would be pulled along behind until it snagged an enemy vessel on the surface (Q).

The "Boat-Fish"

In the late 1700s, factories were springing up all over England. **Raw materials** and finished products had to be transported back and forth. The English built new roadways and canals. Fulton saw his chance for a better life. He wrote to a friend, "I have not painted a picture for more than two years, as I have little doubt but canals will answer my purpose much better."

He spent several years working on canals. He also kept inventing things. One was a special saw to cut marble. Another was a better way of making rope. For some reason, he decided to go to France in 1797.

France and England were at war with each other. Fulton didn't like the idea of war. He wanted to invent a weapon to make war even more horrible. If he could do that, he thought, countries would stop fighting each other. This weapon was the "boat-fish." It was a very early version of a submarine.

He launched his little vessel in 1800. He named it *Nautilus* (NAW-tih-luss). It was about 25 feet long. It could stay **submerged** for several hours. Fulton designed *Nautilus* to sneak up on enemy warships. Then it would attach explosives to the hull.

The French said they would pay him for every English ship he sank. He tried a couple of times but didn't succeed. Then the French lost interest.

The British found out about Fulton's submarine. They asked Fulton if he would work on it for them. Fulton agreed. In 1805 British warships defeated the French at the Battle of Trafalgar. The French fleet was no

An English fleet under the command of Admiral Horatio Nelson defeated the French at the Battle of Trafalgar. Hundreds of men lost their lives during the fighting. With the war over, neither France nor England would use Fulton's submarines.

longer a threat. The British also lost interest in the submarine. Soon Fulton himself lost interest. He was already working on another exciting project.

17

Robert Livingston was one of the men who signed the Declaration of Independence. He became Fulton's business partner. He provided the funds to build the *North River Steam Boat*.

Steam

In 1801, Fulton met Robert Livingston. Livingston had signed the Declaration of Independence. When Fulton met him, he was representing the U.S. government in France. He was very wealthy. He had purchased the right to operate steamboats on the Hudson River.

It was easy to go downstream on the Hudson River, because boats could float with the current. It was very difficult to go the other way. Livingston believed that a steamboat could be built to go against the current. It could make a lot of money carrying passengers.

So far, no one had been able to build a steamboat for Livingston. Livingston was very

John Fitch tests his first successful steamboat on the Delaware River in 1787. The steam on this boat drove ranks of straight paddles. Fitch also tried using paddle wheels and screw propellers with his steam engine. One of his ships carried passengers and freight on the Delaware, but he could not make a profit. He died in 1798, five years before Fulton tested his small boat in Paris.

impressed with Fulton. He asked him to try to build one.

Some Americans had already built steamboats. John Fitch made one in 1787, but hardly anyone wanted to ride in it. Fitch became discouraged and gave up on the project.

In 1803, Fulton launched a small steamboat in the Seine (SEN) River in Paris. The test was successful. Now Fulton wanted to return to the United States.

When Fulton came home in 1806, he went to work on his Hudson River steamboat. It was about 140 feet long and nearly 20 feet wide. Fulton mounted a paddle wheel on each side. The paddle wheels would push the boat through the water. Right from the start, it was successful. Fulton became famous.

Thomas Jefferson was the third president of the United States. His Louisiana Purchase in 1803 nearly doubled the size of the United States. The purchase included the mighty Mississippi River.

The Mighty Mississippi

Fulton and Livingston wanted to do even more. Most roads in the United States were not well made. It was hard to transport goods over land. Rivers, though, had many ports. If a steamboat could link those ports, its owners would make a lot of money.

In 1803, President Thomas Jefferson purchased the Louisiana Territory from France. The size of the United States doubled. The Mississippi River was part of the Louisiana Purchase. The river was the key to developing and expanding the new territory.

Fulton designed a new and larger steamer. He called it the *New Orleans* after the port where it would be based. The boat was built in

Pittsburgh. It left in September 1811. There were many **obstacles** in the river. There was even a major earthquake. Nothing stopped the boat. It arrived safely in New Orleans. It covered more than 1,500 miles in less than four months.

Soon Fulton and Livingston had more than a dozen steamboats in operation. The partnership was doing very well financially. Fulton had become a rich man.

Their success attracted many **competitors**. The partners spent a lot of time in court trying to defend their earnings from these competitors.

Livingston died in 1813. With his partner gone, Fulton was busier than ever.

Meanwhile, the United States had declared war on England in 1812. Fulton became interested again in weapons of war. He built the *Fulton I,* a huge steam-powered warship. The war ended before the ship could be used.

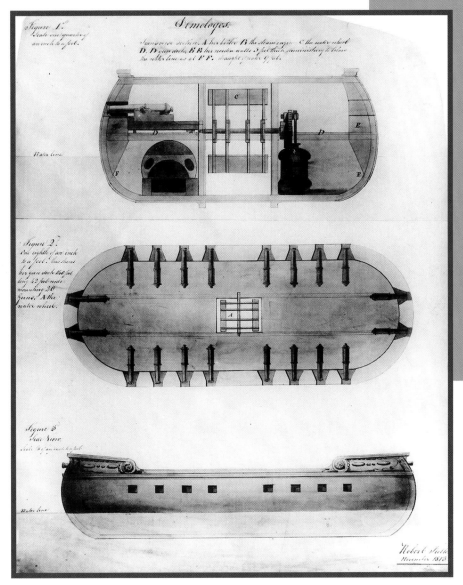

Several views of the *Fulton I*. Fulton intended for it to become the first steam-powered warship. The paddle wheel (A) was in a slot in the ship, well protected by the hull and ranks of cannons.

The U.S. Navy completed *Fulton I* after Robert Fulton died. Sailors lived on it in the New York Harbor at the Brooklyn Navy Yard. In 1829, a gunpowder explosion destroyed the ship.

The ship indirectly caused Fulton's own end. Early in 1815, he stopped by the shipyard where workers were servicing the ship. Then he headed home with his lawyer, Robert Emmet. Emmet fell through some ice.

Fulton helped pull him out. He became severely chilled from the cold water. A few days later, he died. He was just 49. Historians have often wondered what additional inventions he might have developed if he had lived longer.

In 1889, Pennsylvania gave a statue of Robert Fulton to the National Statuary Hall in Washington, D.C. The statue shows Fulton holding a model of the *North River Steam Boat.*

CHRONOLOGY

1765 Robert Fulton is born on November 14 in Pennsylvania.

1774 Robert Fulton's father dies.

1783 Robert moves to Philadelphia and works with a jeweler.

1786 He moves to England to study painting.

1797 He moves to France during the war between France and England.

1800 He successfully tests *Nautilus* submarine.

1801 Fulton meets Robert Livingston. They become partners.

1803 Fulton successfully tests his steamboat on Seine River in Paris, France.

1806 He returns to the United States.

1807 He makes a successful run up the Hudson River on the *North River Steam Boat*.

1808 He marries Harriet Livingston.

1810 He designs Mississippi riverboat, the *New Orleans*.

1813 He designs steam-powered warship *Fulton I*.

1815 Robert Fulton dies in New York City on February 23.

1889 A statue of Fulton is given to the National Statuary Hall to represent the state of Pennsylvania.

TIMELINE IN HISTORY

1698 Thomas Savery patents the first practical steam engine.

1711 English inventor Thomas Newcomen installs the first commercially successful steam engine.

1769 James Watt invents an improved version of Newcomen's engine.

1775 The Revolutionary War begins.

1783 The Revolutionary War ends.

1787 John Fitch launches his successful steamship on the Delaware River.

1801 Richard Trevithick invents the first steam-powered locomotive.

1812 The War of 1812 begins; it ends early in 1815.

1819 The American ship *Savannah* becomes the first steamship to cross the Atlantic Ocean.

1830 *Tom Thumb,* first steam locomotive in the United States, transports 40 passengers at more than 10 miles an hour.

1843 SS *Great Britain* becomes first steam-powered, iron-hulled passenger ship.

1862 The USS *Monitor* and the CSS *Virginia* fight the world's first naval battle between warships powered entirely by steam.

1869 The transcontinental railroad is completed.

FIND OUT MORE

Books

Bowen, Andy Russell. *A Head Full of Notions: A Story about Robert Fulton.* Minneapolis: Carolrhoda Books, 1997.

Ford, Carin T. *Robert Fulton: The Steamboat Man.* Berkeley Heights, New Jersey: Enslow Publishers, 2004.

Gillis, Jennifer Blizen. *Robert Fulton.* Chicago: Heinemann, 2004.

Landau, Elaine. *Robert Fulton.* New York: Franklin Watts, 1991.

Schaefer, Lola M. *Robert Fulton.* Mankato, Minnesota: Capstone Press, 2000.

Works Consulted

Morgan, John S. *Robert Fulton.* New York: Mason/Charter, 1977.

Philip, Cynthia Owen. *Robert Fulton, a Biography.* New York: Franklin Watts, 1985.

Sale, Kirkpatrick. *The Fire of His Genius: Robert Fulton and the American Dream.* New York: The Free Press, 2001.

On the Internet

Dickinson, H. W. "Robert Fulton: Engineer and Artist," London, 1913, http://www.history.rochester.edu/steam/dickinson/

MIT Inventor of the Week Archive: "Robert Fulton,"
http://web.mit.edu/invent/iow/fulton.html
"The North River Steam Ship Clermont,"
http://www.kiac-usa.com/clermont.html

GLOSSARY

competitors (kum-PEH-tih-turs)—People who go up against one another in a race to win.

era (AYR-uh)—A time period during which an important series of events occurs.

estate (ih-STAYT)—A large area of property on which a luxurious house is built.

folly (FAH-lee)—Foolishness.

obstacles (OB-stih-kuls)—Things that get in the way.

raw materials (RAH muh-TEE-ree-uls)—Natural substances such as cotton or wood that are used to make finished products.

skyrocket (SKYE-rah-kit)—A type of fireworks that soars into the air and then explodes into a series of colors.

submerged (sub-MURJD)—Completely under the water.

INDEX